Berkeley

Berkeley

The Life and Spirit
of a Remarkable Town

—◦—

Photographs by Kiran Singh

Text by Ellen Weis

Frog, Ltd.
Berkeley, California

Half-title page: The pedestrian/cycle bridge over Interstate 80 leading to Aquatic Park. *Title-page:* A view of Berkeley from the Bay. *Right:* The Campanile at U.C. Berkeley glows at night. *Contents page:* Mosaic tile on the sidewalk in the arts district.

Compilation copyright © 2004 by Frog, Ltd.

Photographs copyright © 2004 by Kiran Singh

Text copyright © 2004 by Ellen Weis

Foreword by Michael Chabon copyright © 2002 by Michael Chabon. Originally published by *Gourmet*. All rights reserved. Reprinted by arrangement with Mary Evans Inc.

See p. 120 for permissions and acknowledgments

Published by Frog, Ltd.

Frog, Ltd. books are distributed by North Atlantic Books, P.O. Box 12327, Berkeley, California 94712.

Book and cover design by Brad Greene, Greene Design

Printed in Singapore

North Atlantic Books' publications are available through most bookstores. For further information, call 800-337-2665 or visit our website at www.northatlanticbooks.com.

Substantial discounts on bulk quantities are available to corporations, professional associations, and other organizations. For details and discount information, contact our special sales department.

Library of Congress Cataloguing-in-Publication Data

Singh, Kiran. 1951–
Berkeley : the life and spirit of a remarkable town / photographs by Kiran Singh ; commentary by Ellen Weis.
     p. cm.
  ISBN 1-58394-093-6 (pbk.)
  1. Berkeley (Calif.)—Pictorial works. 2. Berkeley (Calif.)—Description and travel. 3. Berkeley (Calif.)—Social life and customs. 4. Architecture—California—Berkeley—Pictorial works. 5. Berkeley (Calif.)—Buildings, structures, etc.—Pictorial works. I. Weis, Ellen, 1957– II. Title.

F869.B5S56 2004
979.4'67'0222—dc22

                                                     2004047194
                                                           CIP

1 2 3 4 5 6 7 8 9 TWP 09 08 07 06 05 04

Contents

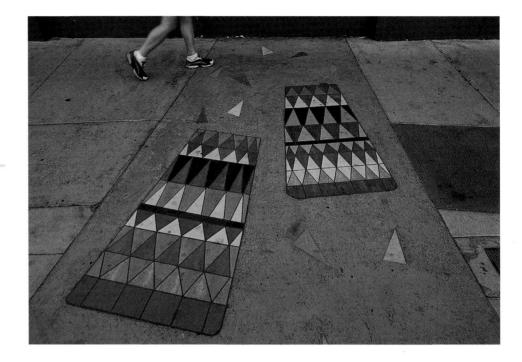

The Mysteries of Berkeley

by Michael Chabon

Where passion is married to intelligence, you may find genius, neurosis, madness, or rapture. None of these is really an unfamiliar presence in the tree-lined streets of Berkeley, California. For a city of one hundred thousand people—toss in another thirty thousand to account for the transient population of the University—we have more than our share of geniuses. The town, to be honest, is lousy with them. Folklorists, chefs, tattoo artists, yogis, guitarists, biologists of the housefly, GUI theorists, modern masters of algebra, Greil Marcus: we have geniuses in every field and discipline. As for neurosis, you can pretty much start at my house and work your way outward in any direction. Obsession, fixation, phobia, hypochondriasis, self-flagellation, compulsive confession of weakness and wrong doing, repetition mania, chronic recrimination, and second-guessing—from parents of toddlers, to fanatical collectors of wax recordings by Turkish klezmer bands of the 1920s, to non-eaters of anything white or which respires, to that august tribunal of collective neurosis, the Berkeley City Council: if neuroses were swimming pools one might, like Cheever's swimmer, steer a course from my house to the city limits and never touch dry land. Madness: a painful thing, which it does not do to romanticize. But it seems to me that among the many sad and homeless people who haunt Berkeley one finds an unusually high number of poets, sages, secret Napoleons, and old-fashioned prophets of doom. The mentally ill citizens of Berkeley read, as they kill a winter afternoon in the warmth of the public library; they generate theories, which they will share; they sell their collected works out of a canvas tote bag. As for rapture, it is harder to observe first-

ABOVE

Tile wall at Martin Luther King Park.

OPPOSITE

Octopus kites soar near the water at César Chávez Park.

hand, and is furthermore something that people, even people in Berkeley, do not necessarily care to discuss. But Berkeley is rich with good places to be rapt: at the eyepiece of an electron microscope or a cloud chamber, at a table at Chez Panisse, in a yoga room, under a pair of headphones at Amoeba Records, in Tilden Park, in the great disorderly labyrinth of Serendipity Books, on the dance floor at Ashkenaz while the ouds jangle and the pipes skirl, in a seat at the Pacific Film Archive watching *Kaidan* (Japan, 1965). I'd be willing to bet that, pound for pound, Berkeley is the most enraptured city in America on a daily basis.

If that statement has the ring of boosterism, then permit me to clarify my feelings on the subject of my adopted home: this town drives me crazy. Nowhere else in America are so many people obliged to suffer more inconvenience for the common good. Nowhere else is the individual encumbered with a greater burden of shame and communal disapproval for having intruded, however innocently, on the sensibilities of another. Berkeley's streets, though a rational 19th-century grid underlies them, are a speed-busting tangle of artificial dead ends, obligatory left turns, and deliberately tortuous obstacle-course barriers known as chicanes, put in place to protect children—who are never (God forbid!) sent to play outside. Municipal ordinances intended to protect the nobility of labor in Berkeley's attractive old industrial district steadfastly prevent new-economy businesses from taking over the aging brick-and-steel structures—leaving them empty cenotaphs to the vanished noble laborer of other days. People in the grocery store, meanwhile, have the full weight of Berkeley society behind them as they take it upon themselves to scold you for exposing your child to known allergens or imposing on her your own indisputably negative view of the universe. Passersby feel empowered—indeed, they feel duty-bound—to criticize your parking technique, your failure to sort your recycling into brown paper and white, your resource-hogging four-wheel-drive vehicle, your use of a pinch-collar to keep your dog from straining at the leash.

When Berkeley does not feel like some kind of vast exercise in collective dystopia—a kind of left-wing Plymouth Plantation in which a man may be pilloried for over-illuminating his house at Christmastime—then paradoxically it often feels like a place filled with people incapable of feeling or acting in concert with each other. It is a city of potters and amateur divines, of people so intent on cultivating their own gardens, researching their own theories, following their own bliss, marching to their own drummers, and dancing to the tinkling of their own finger-cymbals that they take no notice of one another at all, or would certainly prefer not to, if it could somehow be arranged. People keep chickens in Berkeley—there are two very loud henhouses within a block of my house. There may be no act more essentially Berkeley than deciding that the rich flavor and healthfulness, the simple, forgotten pleasure of fresh eggs in the morning outweighs the unreasonable attachment of one's immediate neighbors to getting a good night's sleep.

The result, perhaps inevitable, of this paralysis of good intentions, this ongoing, floating opera of public disapproval and the coming into conflict of competing visions of the path to personal bliss, is a populace inclined to kvetching and to the wearing of the default Berkeley facial expression, the suspicious frown. Bliss is, after all, so near at hand; the perfect egg, a good night's sleep, reconciliation with one's mother or the Palestinians, a theory to account for the surprising lack of dark matter in the universe, a radio station that does not merely parrot the lies of government flaks and corporate media outlets—such things can often feel so eminently possible here, given the intelligence and the passion of the citizens. And yet they continue to elude us. Who is responsible? Is it us? Is it you? What are you doing, there, anyway? Don't you know the recycling truck won't take aluminum foil?

So much for boosterism. And yet I declare, unreservedly and with all my heart, that I love Berkeley, California. I can't imagine living happily anywhere else. And all of the things that drive me crazy are the very things that make this town worth knowing, worth putting up with, worth loving and working to preserve.

Part of the charm of Berkeley lies in her setting: the shimmer and eucalyptus sting of the hills on a dusty summer afternoon, hills whose rocky bones jut through the skin of Berkeley in odd outcroppings like Indian Rock; the morning fogs of the flatlands along the Bay, with their smell of mud and their magically vanishing glimpses of Alcatraz and towers of San Francisco. But I have lived in places, from the Puget Sound to the Hudson Valley, from Laguna Beach to Key West, that rivaled if not surpassed Berkeley in spectacular weather, thrilling vistas, and variety of terrain. Not, perhaps, all at the same time, but to greater extremes of beauty. And yet a city with a beautiful site is about as reliably interesting as a person with a beautiful face, and just about as likely to have been spoiled.

Laid atop her remarkable setting between hills and bay, less consistently fine but at its best no less charming, is the built environment of Berkeley. The town, though laid out in the 1880s, boomed in the aftermath of the 1906 earthquake and fire, when it was settled by refugees from San Francisco, fleeing hither under the mistaken impression that the jutting rock ribs of Berkeley's hills would be proof against temblors. The town grew explosively, to its borders, in the twenty years that followed, and as a result the archi-tecture, especially that of her houses, has a pleasing uniformity of variation, with styles ranging from Prairie school to Craftsman to the vari-ous flavors of Spanish. There is even a local style—I live in an exemplar, built in 1907—called the Berkeley Brown Shingle, which combines elements of the Craftsman and the Stick: overhanging eaves, square-pillared porches, elaborate mullions, and built-in cabinetry, the whole enveloped in a rustic skin of the eponymous cedar or redwood shakes. It's a sober style, at least in conception, boxy and grave and appropriately professorial, and yet after decades of benign neglect and dreaminess and the ministrations of an unstintingly benevolent climate, the houses tend to be wildly overgrown with rose vines, wisteria, jasmine, trumpetvine, and outfitted top and sides with unlikely modifications: Zen dormers, orgone

porches, Lemurian observatories. Certain of her streets offer endless instruction in the rich and surprising expressiveness of brown, houses the color of brown beer, of brown bread, of tobacco, a dog's eyes, a fallen leaf, an old upright piano. The harmoniousness of Berkeley's streets and houses is far from perfect—there are tons of hideous concrete-and-aluminum dingbat monstrosities, in particular around the University, and downtown is a hodgepodge of doughty old California commercial structures, used car lots and a few truly lamentable late-60s office towers. But even the most down-at-heel and ill-used streets offer a promise of green shade in the summertime, and many neighborhoods are densely populated by trees, grand old plantations of maple and oak, long rows of ornamental plums that blossom in the winter, persimmon trees, Meyer lemon trees, palm trees and fig trees, monkey puzzles and Norfolk island pines, redwoods and Monterey pines nearly a hundred years old. One of the remarkable things about Berkeley is that, in spite of its decided inferiority to its great neighbor across the Bay in clout, preeminence, population, notoriety, and fame, it has never seemed to dwell in San Francisco's shadow (unlike poor old Oakland down the road). I believe that this may be in part due to the fact that when it comes to trees—a necessary component, in my view, of the greatness of a city—the Colossus of the West can't hold a candle to Berkeley.

But houses and tree plantations, like hills and foggy mudflats, are no reliable guarantors of the excellence of a place to live. That elusive quality always lies, ultimately, in the citizenry; in one's neighbors. And it is ultimately the people of Berkeley—those same irritating frowners and scolders, those very neurotic geniuses and rapt madwomen—who make this place, who ring an endless series of variations on its great theme of personal and communal exploration, and who, above all, fight tooth and nail to hang on to what they love about it.

If there were a hundred good small cities in America fifty years ago—towns built to suit the people who settled them, according to their tastes, aspirations, and the sovereign peculiarities of landscape and weather—today there are no more than twenty-five. In ten years, as the inexorable lattice of sprawl replicates and proliferates, and the downtowns become malls, and the malls downtowns, and the rich syllabary of mercantile America is reduced to a simple alphabet composed of a Blockbuster, a Target, a Starbucks, a Barnes and Noble, a Gap, and a T.G.I.Fridays, and California herself is drowned in a sea of red-tile roofs from San Ysidro to Yreka, there may be fewer than ten. When the end finally comes, I believe that Berkeley will be the last town in America with the ingrained perversity to hold onto its idea of itself. This is a town—on the edge of the country, on the edge of the twenty-first century, on the edge of subducting plates and racial divides and an immense sea of corporate homogeneity—where you can still sign for your groceries at the store around the corner. A Berkeley grocer is a man who preserves such an archaic custom not in spite of the fact but exactly because it's an out-moded and cumbersome way of running a business.

It's in the quirky, small businesses of Berkeley, in fact, places like the old soda fountain in the Elmwood Pharmacy, Alkebulalian Books (specializing in books on the African dias-pora), d.b.a. Brown Records (just on the Oakland side of the city limits), or the Sound Well (used and vintage hi-fi and stereo equipment) that the tensions of Berkeley living, the competing claims on the heart of a Berkeleyite to follow one's

bliss but at the same time to reach a hand out into the void and feel another set of fingers taking hold of one's own, are resolved. These are not merely retail establishments, poor cousins of Rite-Aid, Borders, Sam Goody's, and Circuit City. They are shrines to the classic Berkeley impulse to latch on to something tiny but crucial—the warm sound provided by vacuum tube amplifiers, the mid-60s sides of Ornette Coleman, the African roots of Jesus Christ and his teachings, or a perfectly constructed Black-and-White (with an extra three inches in the steel blender cup)—and pursue it with a mounting sense of self-discovery. And yet they are also, accidentally but fundamentally, gathering places; they all have counters at which the lonely amateur of Coleman or Marantz, the student of Martin Bernal, can pull up a stool and find him- or herself in the company of sym-pathetic minds. Berkeley is richer than any place I've ever lived, in these non-alcoholic taverns of the soul, these unofficial clubhouses of the odd-ball and outré. And it seems as if every year another one pops up, at the bottom of Solano Avenue, in a faded brick stretch of San Pablo Avenue, unfranchisable, inexplicable except as a doorway to fulfillment and fellow-ship. A business that would never thrive anywhere else, patronized by people who would never thrive anywhere else, in a city that lives and dies on the passion and intelligence, the madness and rapture, of its citizens.

Michael Chabon
Berkeley, California

OPPOSITE
Studying in the sun on campus.

LEFT
The art deco neon clock on
Shattuck Avenue.

This elegant 300-foot-long bicycle, pedestrian, and wheelchair-friendly overcrossing, dedicated in 2002, links Aquatic Park with the Eastshore State Park and Marina, across nine busy lanes of Interstate 80.

Downtown

Downtown Berkeley hosts a vital business center, and is the center of city government. Its crown jewel is a growing arts and entertainment district, anchored by two major theater groups, Capoeira Arts Café, and several galleries. Nestled just under the UC Berkeley campus, the district stretches north and south at the top of University Avenue, the long corridor that reaches up from the waterfront and Highway 80. In thirty square blocks, the daytime population includes some 23,000 office workers, 40,000 UC Berkeley graduate and undergraduate students, staff, and faculty, and 3,000 Berkeley High kids. All these people coexist and give the city a pulsing rhythm, punctuated by the underground whistle of the streamlined BART train, which has its main Berkeley stop under Shattuck at Center.

More than 100 restaurants serve an eclectic cuisine from over 15 countries. Five movie theaters boast a total of 21 screens. Award-winning live theater, performance, and dance—with Zellerbach Playhouse just to the west on campus—accompany a lively music and jazz scene. Dozens of specialty retail stores support a dynamic commercial life.

Downtown's main street, Shattuck Avenue, named for early landowner Francis Kittredge Shattuck, was a lively thoroughfare even before Berkeley's incorporation in 1878. Downtown rail access began in 1876, and in 1903 the Key System electric trains were established. BART came along in 1972, with its distinctive glass rotunda station entrance.

ABOVE INSET

The Beaux-Arts City Hall was built in 1908 by Blackwell and Brown. It is now the home of Berkeley Unified School District.

RIGHT

The pink Shattuck Hotel, built in 1909 in Mediterranean Renaissance Revival style, sits to the right of the newly restored public library on Kittredge Street.

The art deco Main Library was completed in 1931 by Berkeley architect James Plachek. In 2002 residents celebrated its reopening after expansion and earthquake retrofitting.

CLOCKWISE FROM THE TOP

High, round classical arches grace the 1915 Post Office building, with friezes, medallions, and wave patterns. • *Earth Song*, a 42-foot-high, deep-red painted steel sculpture by Berkeley resident Po Shu Wang, stands across from the BART plaza. The interactive tuning fork is set to vibrate approximately one million pedestrians each year. • After the 1989 Loma Prieta quake, Berkeley built a new Public Safety Building to house its emergency communication center, which can withstand a 7.0 earthquake.

ABOVE

The Berkeley YMCA has operated
since 1910. A large modern wing was
added in 1994.

RIGHT

Artist Dmitry Drudsky's *Bench Bear*
mosaic bench in the arts district.

CLOCKWISE FROM TOP

Bira Almeida's Capoeira Arts Café, Berkeley Repertory, Aurora Theatre, and the Jazz School all comprise the Addison Street Arts District, designed by the city in 1991.

Shoppers peruse, stroll, sample, and socialize, enjoying being able to buy organic produce, bread, flowers, and related products directly from growers.

$3.25
per pound

Lighten Your Spirit
treat yourself
to the most
perfect peach
in the world

Peaches delight at the Farmer's Market, held downtown next to Martin Luther King Park each Saturday, and Tuesdays at Dwight-Derby Park. Berkeley's involvement in the organic food movement has grown since the 1970s, when Alice Waters and other chefs and restaurateurs created California Cuisine, which became an international phenomenon.

This wall art graces the Arts District a block from Berkeley High. It is one of many touches that bring the visual arts into a performing space.

ABOVE

A view of a new wing of Berkeley High on the east, looking to City Hall, shows the juxtaposition of school and city administration buildings.

RIGHT

One of the few high schools in the nation located in the core of a downtown, Berkeley High holds 3,000 students, who bring creativity, achievement, and youthfulness daily to downtown. The campus includes a core 1922 art deco building with WPA bas-relief sculptures.

ABOVE

Dedicated in 1950, Berkeley Community Theatre
is a round, 3,500-seat art deco auditorium.
Performers have included Joan Baez, Bob Dylan,
the Grateful Dead, Led Zeppelin, Joni Mitchell,
Van Morrison, Jimi Hendrix, and Alanis Morissette.

BISHOP BERKELEY

BERKELEY WAS NAMED IN 1866 by one of the
founders of the University of California,
after Bishop George Berkeley, the 17th-cen-
tury philosopher and writer born in Ireland.
Bishop Berkeley's poem *On the Prospect of
Planting Arts and Learning in America* had a
line quoted often to encourage the
settlement of the West:

> *"Westward the course of empire
> takes its way."*

Berkeley spent only four years in New
England, and died 125 years before his
namesake city was titled. The name stuck.
The poem's first line appears on the city's
seal with a portrait of the Bishop. May 24 is
George Berkeley Day, when everyone is
asked to use the traditional English pronun-
ciation: "Barclay" or "Bark-lee" for that day.

22

Telegraph Avenue

*T*he Haight-Ashbury of Berkeley, Telegraph is
necessarily collegiate, as a main corridor for
students walking to class. It's a mecca for the
young and the young at heart with its college
shops, record stores (Rasputin's, Amoeba), new
and used bookstores, and varied restaurants.
Blake's sponsors rock music and Cody's offers author
readings, kids hang out, students and politicos
hover over coffee at the Med. Not a mall, Telegraph
has historically been a home to creativity and
artistry, homeless people and their dogs, crafts
people with their wares, punk (or beat or flapper)
kids, and college ambience, whatever the decade.

LEFT

Lively characters and cycling students
prove "all the world's a stage" on
Telegraph. Dark glasses, beads, and a
tutu on one bearded gent fit right in
on this boulevard of the exceptional.

BELOW

Every weekend, and at Christmas,
Telegraph Avenue becomes a thriving
bazaar with unique handmade crafts
and apparel.

LEFT INSET

A masked lady and newspaper dress mannequin from Mars Mercantile stare out amid reflections.

OPPOSITE

Originally specializing in the blues, Blake's audiences for 64 years have "discovered" such musical stars as Robert Cray, Cake, Third Eye Blind, Box Set, and other major talents.

ABOVE

An 1890 postcard proclaims the free-spiritedness that has always distinguished Berkeley.

THE STORY OF PEOPLE'S PARK

WHEN THE UNIVERSITY **purchased and tore down community housing with a plan to build athletic fields, protests erupted. The University delayed building the fields, and The Berkeley Barb called for people to come and build a "People's Park." A flurry of excited activity commenced, as people built flowerbeds, dug up soil, and built benches, hopeful of having a community park. A month later the park was bulldozed, protest erupted, and Governor Reagan called in the National Guard. The Park of 1969 lives on in peoples' memories, while today it's a quieter place. It will always remain a symbol of strong town-gown politics.**

RIGHT

Every college town has too many pizza joints. Blondie's has survived decades of craziness as a cheap-eat and a place to people-watch.

BELOW

At the Telegraph Street Fair the avenue closes to traffic and vendors get the whole two blocks, with room for booths, a parade, and general festivity.

ABOVE INSET

Moe's four-story refuge of new and used books is a delight to browsers. Berkeley readers bring in box loads to sell or trade.

LEFT

Cody's has pioneered in-store readings and been on the forefront of the preservation of independent bookstores. Founded in 1956 by Fred and Pat Cody and owned now by Andy Ross, it is one of the most prominent booksellers in the country.

Southside

The South Campus area became known to the nation during the 1960s and early '70s as the setting of student demonstrations and protests. But either side of Telegraph Avenue shows glimpses of the quieter pace of life south of campus around the turn of the century. Claremont encompasses the graceful homes along Piedmont Avenue and above College. Brown shingles, Stick-Eastlake cottages, and Queen Annes spill down to Shattuck—amid middle and elementary schools, a bed and breakfast, restaurants, retail businesses, and the park next to Willard School, which in the '70s was named Ho Chi Minh Park.

RIGHT

St. Mark's Episcopal Church on Bancroft Way at Ellsworth was designed by William Curlett, who created this beautiful Mission Revival church in 1901 with flanking bell towers and a curved españada gable.

The Swedish Mission Church was built in 1907 to reach the large population of Swedish-speaking families in Berkeley. It has been owned and beautifully restored by the New Light Baptist Church since the early 1980s.

LEFT

The Thai Temple holds a brunch feast on Sundays to support its cultural activities and language classes. Spicy aromas, gongs and bells, and strong Thai iced coffee and tea delight under colorful tents.

LEFT

A gaggle of shirts and caps create color at the Ashby Flea Market, a year-round festival of international crafts, vinyl records, jewelery, tools, and surprising kitsch.

LEFT

The Starry Plough, a 30-year-old pub, hosts Irish music, *ceili* dancing, and the weekly Berkeley Poetry Slam contests.

RIGHT

Great world-fare food is served from hippie vans amid clouds of incense and music at the Flea Market, held at the Ashby BART station each weekend.

POETRY IN BERKELEY

SINCE KENNETH REXROTH **held court on the newly founded KPFA in 1949, Berkeley has been a mecca for poets. The Berkeley Renaissance group included Robert Duncan and Jack Spicer. Allen Ginsberg finished "Howl" on Milvia Street, and Gary Snyder, Phillip Whalen, and Lew Welch met in a cottage in Berkeley and were immortalized by Jack Kerouac in *Dharma Bums*.**

In the '60s Robert Hawley began Oyez Press. The Berkeley Poetry Conference at the University brought Black Mountain poets Charles Olson and Robert Creeley westward in 1965; Alta's Shameless Hussy Press and Judy Grahn's *Edward the Dyke* pioneered feminist presses. Ntozake Shange first performed "for colored girls who have considered suicide/when the rainbow is enuf" at the Bacchanal, a women's bar on Solano.

Poetry at Cody's weekly readings began in 1972, and Joyce Jenkins (pictured above) moved *Poetry Flash* to Berkeley in 1978. The West Coast Print Center printed many literary magazines, while Small Press Distribution began distribution to bookstores. The Language Poets emerged from Berkeley in the '70s. Readings, lit mags, fanzines, poetry slams, and hip-hop poetry: poetry in Berkeley will keep on being lively.

ABOVE

James LeBrecht and artist Nanette Tver hang out near the Center for Independent Living. Curb-cut sidewalks made Berkeley wheelchair accessible years before others cities followed suit.

Malcom X, a 4th–6th grade elementary school, serves both hill and flatlands populations, sending students on to middle school, Berkeley High, and various private schools. • The Black Repertory Group was founded in 1964 and opened its new theater in 1987. A 250-seat main stage provides rehearsal space, with special emphasis on youth workshops.

LEFT

A worker neatens up produce at Berkeley Bowl. Popular for its unusual produce and good fish, the Bowl retains many customers who move outside of Berkeley, its vast new quarters still crowded with discriminating shoppers.

BELOW

Skaters of all ages enjoy Iceland, opened in 1940 to give city residents a chance to swirl and twirl, play ice hockey, practice school figures, and socialize.

OPPOSITE

La Peña, which means gathering place, was founded in 1975 as a center for cultural exchange. Latin food complements international music, dance, theater, kids' programs, and rotating art exhibits.

FROM THE TOP

Part of the public library system, the Tool Lending Library lends about 5,000 tools a year free to Berkeley residents. Neighboring Temescal and San Francisco have established similar programs, two decades later. • Remodelers love the outdoor yard at the Urban Ore Ecopark, full of doors, windows, sinks, bathtubs, and yard ornaments for the do-it-yourselfer or contractor. • A hoary owl keeps watch at Urban Ore's new quarters, where searching out old photos, furniture, books, etc. is a pleasure.

ABOVE

A mural on a south-facing brick wall at Ashby and Martin Luther King near the BART station.

LEFT

For 30 years until his death in 2002, Mr. Charles stood on his porch near Oregon and Martin Luther King Streets and waved to morning drivers, bringing spirit and good humor.

The Elmwood

As the Gold Rush brought wealthy settlers to the East Bay, entrepreneurs like the Ashby brothers developed orchards and ranches in the rolling hills of what is now the Elmwood. This country area was annexed to the city of Berkeley in 1891, and soon real estate agents began touting it as the closest neighborhood to Telegraph Avenue and the newly-forming university.

A growth spurt of elegant homes accompanied the new Key System of streetcars on the College Avenue route, a lively commercial district. The Elmwood has retained its pedestrian-friendly, old-world charm for 100 years.

OPPOSITE

Gracious houses and gardens, like this one on Benvenue fill the neighborhoods on either side of College and Ashby.

LEFT INSET

For more than 90 years, Berkeley residents and visitors have shopped College Avenue, which hosts a local movie theater, hardware store, pet store, toy store, soda fountain, ethnic restaurants, and jewelry, clothing, and craft boutiques.

A landmark built in 1915 whose spires are
visible from four counties, the Claremont
Hotel and Spa offers 10 tennis courts, gardens,
restaurants, an Olympic-sized pool, and a
newly renovated luxurious day spa.

ABOVE

Eclectic houses in all neighborhoods,
including the Elmwood, contribute to
a village atmosphere.

RIGHT

Sidewalk cafes allow patio eating
most of the year on College, which
has an astonishing variety of
restaurants. Sidewalk strollers are
happy, too.

OZZIE'S

THE HEART OF THE ELMWOOD has been the corner Elmwood Pharmacy and Soda Fountain, pictured above in the 1950s. The vintage lunch counter and red-vinyl stools date from the second owner, Fred Beretta, who gave the neighborhood a place to socialize with cream sodas, phosphates, and egg creams.

In 1950 WWII veteran pilot Charles Osborne bought the pharmacy. Ozzie's soda fountain blossomed for three decades, serving families, artists (Richard Diebenkorn and Elmer Bischoff), Berkeley Rep actors, and Jane Fonda. Ozzie's was a place of lively political debate and neighborhood petitions: in the early 1950s neighbors stopped the Elmwood from being decimated by the newly planned freeway. In 1981 another grass-roots effort saved Elmwood shops from destruction by outside commercial development. Ozzie's is intact today, serving up sandwiches, homemade soups, and amiable conversation.

45

Campus

The University's flagship campus ranks nationally in the number of graduate programs in the top ten of their fields. Graduate and undergraduate students come to the professional schools, joint programs with UCSF, and The College of Liberal Arts and Sciences (L&S). Although Berkeley is famous for the upheaval of the Free Speech Movement in the late '60s and subsequent student protest movements, the daily life of an undergraduate involves sports, arts, fraternities, sororities, a wide diversity of social and political clubs, and—oh yes, studying.

ABOVE

The Medallion at Sather Gate reads FIAT LUX, "Let There Be Light," the motto of the University of California. It rests atop a patinaed bronze arch. Since the Free Speech Movement it has been a symbol of the fact that learning is not only in the classroom, and that student activism is a vital part of a democratic society.

RIGHT

The distinctive red roof tiles and copper skylights of Cal's campus buildings draw from the architectural style of California Missions.

A guitarist plays at Sather Gate. Music abounds on campus, from spontaneous drumming near The Bear's Lair to formal concerts at Zellerbach Playhouse and Theater. • A couple strikes up a tango in front of Sproul Plaza. • A student about to cross one of the creeks that flow through campus.

Sather Tower was completed in 1914 by John Galen Howard. The 307-foot-tall Beaux-Arts monolith soars above the classrooms, laboratories, and libraries of campus, as if to represent the triumph of scholarship.

Sather Gate at Dusk, 1939, a watercolor by Chiura Obata, shows a thoughtful student returning home amid the bustle of Telegraph Avenue.

Berkeley African Students Association is one of 250 organizations that are part of the Associated Students of the University of California. BASA has been around since the early 1960s, and stays active on Sproul Plaza.

The Reflecting Pool in Memorial Glade is dedicated to the memory of Cal alumni who served in World War II. Its contemplative beauty offers students and faculty a meditative setting for services. The largest crowd since the '60s honored victims of September 11, 2001.

A peace lamp floats in the waters at a Peace Vigil at the Estuary, Aquatic Park.

THE FREE SPEECH MOVEMENT

DURING THE FALL OF 1964 students returning from civil rights actions in the South looked forward to recruitment and fundraising on campus. They encountered prohibitions from the 1950s McCarthy era of anti-communism on leafletting, fundraising, setting up tables, and "orating." Several groups defied the rules and set up card tables; they were met with a ban on any kind of political activity. Empowered by membership in Students for a Democratic Society and Student Non-Violent Coordinating Committee, Berkeley students demanded an end to the regulation of political activity on campus—i.e. free speech. Rallies, protests, sit-ins, and a student strike followed, as students began to rethink their world and critique University governance. Mario Savio, a junior, became a hero for his ability to voice feelings about student powerlessness. He helped Berkeley students, faculty, and administrators understand the necessity of students participating in the larger political world.

University House, home to the University's Chancellor. The four-story mansion has seen a spectrum of formal events, including visits by Presidents Theodore Roosevelt, Wilson, and Kennedy, as well as occasional protests over inadequate student housing and budget cuts.

Students walk among a miniature "Avenue of the Giants" in the middle of campus—a serene Redwood Grove near classroom buildings and libraries.

ABOVE

Berkeley's Haas School of Business has turned out scores of successful business men and women during its 100+ years. The new campus is designed around a spacious courtyard.

TOP RIGHT

Much of the University was developed under the philanthropic sponsorship of the Hearst family. Architect Julia Morgan worked with Bernard Maybeck to create the Beaux-Arts Hearst Gymnasium. Morgan built three pools with onlooking goddess statues and marble decking.

BELOW RIGHT

Students walk by the distinctively gnarled London plane trees, which have complemented the classical architecture since 1915.

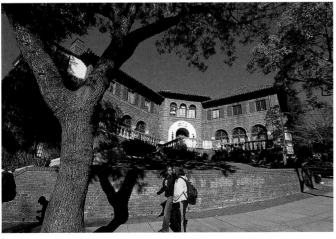

ABOVE

Strawberry Creek was a primary reason the founding trustees chose to build the University on this naturally idyllic site. This footbridge on the north side provides a gentle transition for walks between campus buildings.

LEFT

The L-shaped Phi Gamma Delta Fraternity house set above Channing Circle on the corner of Piedmont Avenue is a Mediterranean Revival beauty from 1928, designed by architect Frederick Reimers for use as a fraternity.

LEFT

10,000 football partisans gather at the Greek Theater for the annual Bonfire Rally held the Friday before the Big Game between the Stanford Cardinal and the California Bears—a tradition since 1916.

TOP RIGHT

The mural at Edwards Stadium, painted in 1933, is symbolic of Oski, the costumed mascot who replaced live black bear mascots in the 1930s.

RIGHT

Intramural soccer, on the turf at Maxwell Family Field. The castle-like dorm behind is Bowles Hall, built in 1929.

LEFT

Theta Delta Chi Fraternity with its classic, collegiate brick-and-ivy house, is one of many huge mansions from the early 1900s which have housed many generations of Cal students.

RIGHT

When International House opened in 1930, it was the largest student-housing complex in the Bay Area and the first coeducational residence west of the Mississippi. Resident students and scholars from 80 countries know that the I-House boasts one of the best cafés in Berkeley.

NEXT PAGE

Graduating seniors from Berkeley watch Native American Indian dancers at the Hearst Greek Theatre, the 8,500-seat amphitheater designed by campus architect John Galen Howard. The huge round columns have witnessed major concerts, lectures, and events, including appearances by Sarah Bernhardt, the Dalai Lama, and the Grateful Dead.

Hans Hofmann
Scintillating Spaces

LEFT INSET

Edith Kramer, Pacific Film Archive's director, was awarded the Chancellor's Distinguished Service Award for her role in developing the internationally acclaimed organization that archives, preserves, and presents films from all eras and regions of the world.

OPPOSITE

Looking down a ramp at Berkeley Art Museum, which exhibits modern art, including major shows of Rothko, Pollock, Calder, and Helen Frankenthaler. The Hans Hofmann permanent collection of 47 paintings inspired the building's abstract architectural design.

BELOW

The impressive, tubular monel metal sculpture titled *Return to Piraeus* is by influential artist Peter Voulkos, who taught at Cal for almost 30 years.

The French Hotel is a small European-style inn converted from a brick French laundry in the mid '70s. People line up every morning for some of Berkeley's best coffees. Chess players, dogs, and great conversation enliven the Café's sidewalk through dusk.

North Berkeley

N orth Berkeley encompasses residential and retail areas on the north side of campus, and is often called "Northside." It developed after Southern Pacific Railroad was extended to Vine Street in 1878. The commercial center at Shattuck and Vine is now the hub of Berkeley's "foodie" lifestyle, emphasizing organic produce, free-range meat and poultry, and innovative commercial bakeries. Anchored by the fame of Alice Water's Chez Panisse restaurant, the Cheese Board, and the delicatessen Poulet, the area has been called the Gourmet Ghetto for several decades. Pastries, pastas, cheeses, teas, juice smoothies, coffees, and irresistible pizzas reward the palate in this area. Blooming flower stands, coffeehouses, and ethnic eateries make this district a few acres of heaven on earth.

COOPERATIVES AND COLLECTIVES

THE ROCHEDALE **principals of class owner-ship influenced worker-cooperatives around the country in the '30s, and took hold in Berkeley.**

In 1937 about 60 families called The Berkeley Buyers' Club leased a shop on Shattuck Avenue staffed by volunteers, offering recycling and bulk foods. This became Pacific Cooperative Services, and later the Consumers Cooperative of Berkeley. By the 1950s it included a credit union, day care, and insurance. COOP operated three large grocery stores from the 1960s to the late 1980s. Other worker-owned businesses that bloomed in the early '70s were The Cheese Board, Nabolom Bakery, the Juice Bar, Missing Link Bicycle cooperative, Ink Works print shop, and Bookpeople, the alternative book distributor.

ABOVE INSET

The Cheese Board is one of the few remaining worker owned and operated collectives in the country. Worker-ownership and collective decision-making increase worker involvement in quality and superior service.

OPPOSITE

A patron leaves Chez Panisse. Famed restaurateur Alice Waters founded it 32 years ago, starting a tipping point of chefs, restaurant owners, and consumers who embraced organic foods and merged it with elegant cuisine.

OPPOSITE INSET

The Edible Schoolyard garden at Martin Luther King Jr. Middle School was started by Alice Waters. An innovative partnership between the Berkeley School Board and private foundations allows students to learn how to plant, harvest, prepare, and cook organic food they grow themselves.

Monterey Market, at the corner of Hopkins and Monterey, offers aisles of select California produce as well as exotic vegetables and fruits from around the world.

CLOCKWISE FROM THE TOP

Christmas lights and a menorah adorn this Northside home, all dressed up in a place that has no snow for the holidays. Berkeley has a high interfaith marriage rate per capita, and many community programs founded on the richness of diversity. • At the top of Solano Avenue, the art deco sign of the Oaks Theatre is a beacon for cinephiles. Built in 1925, it was saved and restored in the '90s as a classic movie palace—complete with etched glass doors and lobby chandeliers. • A bus emerges from the Solano Tunnel, built originally for light rail commuter trains to San Francisco. At the turn of the century city planners were interested in Berkeley becoming the capital of California. The developers of the Northbrae tract in North Berkeley consequently named many streets after counties: Solano, Colusa, The Alameda, Modoc, Tulare, Los Angeles, Napa, and Yolo.

Berkeley Hills

The Berkeley Hills run from Kensington to the Oakland border. Heavenly views begin with the campus and stadium, and the town of Berkeley, and stretch to the Bay, Marin Hills, Golden Gate Bridge, and San Francisco. Roads wind up to several entrances to Tilden Park in the East Bay Regional Parks District.

Seven creeks run from the hills to the bay—lovely when uncovered, but troublesome as the aging, 60-year-old concrete culverts collapse. Experts favor day-lighting creeks, since open creeks are more capable of channeling flood waters and removing pollutants before they reach the Bay. Eight percent of the city's private property, nearly 2,150 parcels, sits within 30 feet of a creek.

THE ROSE GARDEN

FOR SIXTY-SEVEN YEARS the Berkeley Rose Garden has been a place to watch the sun set over the Golden Gate, to enjoy Mother's Day, and (booked a year in advance) to be married. Built as a WPA project over five years in the mid 1930s, the dramatic, 3.6-acre natural amphitheater boasts 250 varieties of roses in 3,000 bushes, set among six semicircular stone terraces with Cordornices Creek at the bottom. The garden's arc is anchored by redwood pergolas at the top and a viewing platform with sundial.

The Rose Garden is supported by the City and the Friends of the Berkeley Rose Garden, and sits adjacent to tennis courts. Across Euclid Avenue is Codornices Park, with a baseball diamond, basketball courts, a children's playground, and paths above and across the creek. A pedestrian tunnel under Euclid Avenue, perfect for the mysteries of children's play, links park and Rose Garden. The roses reach their peak in May and last through summer, making a perfect setting for rendezvous, dreamy afternoons, or picnics.

ABOVE

Altocumulus clouds create a dramatic backdrop for a view of the pergolas from below in the Rose Garden.

LEFT

A couple relaxes on a bench in the Rose Garden.

A mom walks her baby outside Lawrence Hall of Science, an educational math, science, and natural resources museum for children, featuring hands-on displays and a planetarium. It was named for Ernest Orlando Lawrence, the University's first Nobel laureate.

The Firestorm Community Mural Project at the Rockridge BART station is a wall of 1,000 hand-painted tiles made by Berkeley residents to honor firefighters, survivors, and those who lost their lives in the devastating 1991 Oakland Firestorm.

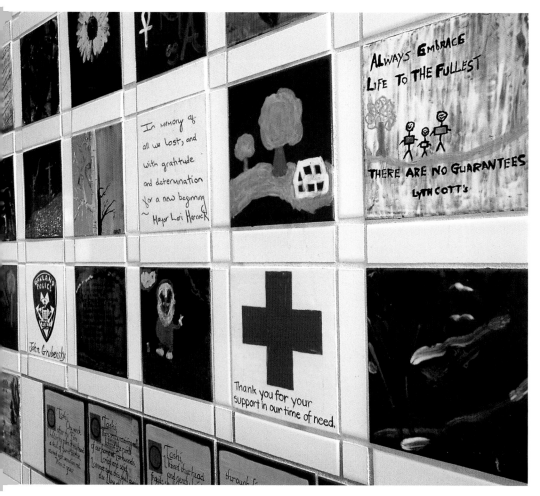

LEFT

Buildings catch the sun at Lawrence Berkeley National Laboratory. "The Rad Lab" is the famous radiation research facility where experiments in 1940 bombarding uranium in the cyclotron yielded plutonium, laying the groundwork for the development of atomic weapons. Named after founding director Ernest O. Lawrence, the lab has employed thousands of scientists, researchers, technicians, and students since 1931.

BELOW

An active Save the Bay group works to alert people in Berkeley that everything you put down a culvert pollutes the Bay.

ABOVE INSET AND RIGHT

Marin Circle's fountain in the daytime, above, and at night, right. The roundabout fountain was Berkeley's first public art installation, completed in 1911. A runaway truck careening down steep Marin Avenue destroyed it in 1958. It was finally replaced in 1996 through the efforts of a strong grassroots neighborhood coalition, which keeps it up and decorates it at Christmas.

A bike rider looks across Tuscan golden hills at Inspiration Point. A favorite for walking and biking, Nimitz Way Trail goes north to Wildcat Canyon Regional Park and overlooks San Pablo Reservoir.

Tilden Park

Tilden Park is the East Bay's great escape. Ten minutes from Campus and central Berkeley, its three major entrances lead to a wildlife habitat, magical redwood and monterey pine groves, lakes, a golf course, an international botanical garden, pony rides, a 740-acre nature area, a petting farm, plus a miniature guage steam train. And miles and miles of trails.

Cattle, sheep, and goats graze in spring and early summer. Each year from November through March, South Park Drive is closed to protect migrating and breeding California newts.

ABOVE INSET

The Little Farm at Tilden Park employs a full-time farmer who tells about the animals. The 1955 barn full of pigs, goats, cows, sheep, rabbits, ducks, and chickens gives kids of all ages a touch of country life.

BELOW INSET

Quiet walks along fire trails—a chance to visit, and a break from the humming city streets below.

THE FOUNDING OF TILDEN

IN THE EARLY 1930s, a far-sighted group of community leaders and urban planners established the East Bay Regional Park District, a "greenbelt" of 100,000 acres where urban growth would not be permitted. Attorney Charles Lee Tilden gave generously to the new park system, and became the first president of its Board of Directors.

Students were employed through the National Youth Administration and the Civilian Conservation Corps to build fire roads, picnic grounds, hiking paths in the 2000-acre park, and Lake Anza's dam and the Golf Course. WPA workers relocated part of the Brazilian exhibit from the 1939 San Francisco Golden Gate Exhibition, which became the "Brazilian Room," a stately stone hall used for weddings and events. Above, a rider in the '50s enjoys the antique carousel and Wurlitzer organ piping just the right tunes.

ABOVE INSET

Real steam, real engines, a friendly conductor. Redwood Valley Railway created a pint-size, twelve-car steam train, which chugs a leisurely 12-minute ride through the redwoods of Tilden, complete with piercing whistles that can be heard for miles.

LEFT INSET

Swimmers frolic in freshwater Lake Anza, with its wide beach for small children and sunbathers, and nine acres for summer swims. In the winter, walking around the lake is a popular activity.

LEFT

A hidden gem in Berkeley is Tilden Park's Golf Course. Set in a fairy tale landscape of fragrant conifers and rolling greens, the fairways inspire golfers of all levels.

West Berkeley

West Berkeley runs south from Albany to Ashby Avenue, and west from above San Pablo Avenue to the Bay. Historic 1860 homes and churches abut warehouses and auto body shops; nurseries, restaurants, and small shops abound. An Indian community of sari shops, food stores, and restaurants cluster around lower University Avenue; a group of San Pablo Avenue shops are called the Left Bank; and surplus yards Omega Salvage and Omega Too delight do-it-yourselfers. Fourth Street and the industrial parks on Heinz Street coexist with "light" industry as more software entrepreneurs, furniture makers, artisans, publishers, and book distributors find Berkeley good for business. Where else can Bayer Biotech and Libby Labs be neighbors with Urban Ore and Good Vibrations?

RIGHT

The l-o-n-g bar at Brennan's Restaurant has served up beer, mixed drinks, and Hof Brau cafeteria food since 1959. It is now run by grandkids Margaret and Barney Wade.

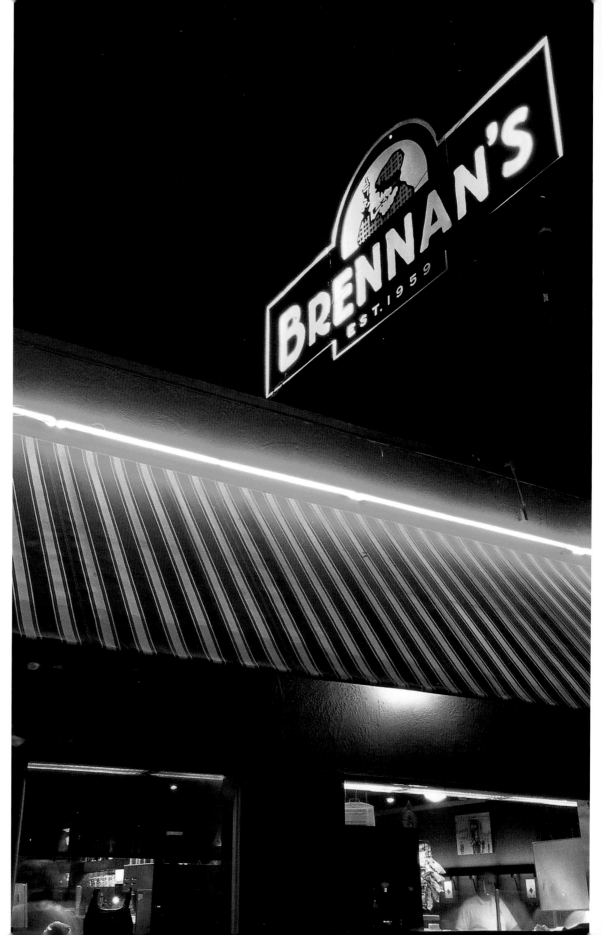

CLOCKWISE FROM THE TOP

Since 1890 Spenger's Fish Grotto has been family-owned. Bud Spenger retired in 1998, but a revitalized Spenger's reopened in 2000 under new management. Great seafood in a family atmosphere amid wild nautical memorabilia.

• *Pablo*, a Mavis McClure bronze, maintains a contemplative posture unfazed by Fourth Street shoppers. • Shoppers from around the Bay enjoy Fourth Street, which blossomed in the early '80s. Careful to mix local independent stores with chains, its gradual growth has made it Berkeley's most successful shopping district.

• A musician entertains on Fourth Street, creating a mellow ambience.

CLOCKWISE FROM THE TOP

On Ninth Street at Hearst, the Charles Bugbee-designed Church of the Good Shepherd is one of the finest "Carpenter Gothic" churches in the East Bay. • Berkeley's 1860s homes have been preserved in the Delaware Street Historic District, including Bowen's Inn, Berkeley's first retail establishment, built by former merchant seaman Captain William Bowen in 1854. • The stucco bungalow, so ubiquitous in Berkeley, often blooms with sumptuous flowering bushes, as here.

OPPOSITE

The quieter haunts of the Oceanview district suit many artists and live-work artisans. Corrugated metal siding and totem poles make a statement here.

THE SETTLING OF OCEAN VIEW

OCEANVIEW'S EARLY SETTLEMENT community was started in 1853 with the establishment of Jacob's Landing (at the foot of Delaware Street) and Bowen's Inn, at Delaware and San Pablo Avenue. Its architectural heart is from Third to Tenth Streets and from University north to Jones Street. Recent research in Indian settlements, creek restoration, and historical ecology has revealed its extensive Ohlone shellmounds and underground creeks; the Victorian "workingmen's cottages" and churches have increased interest in historical preservation. As elsewhere, houses and commercial development increased with the arrival of railroad lines in the 1870s and '80s, peaking in the 1890s. Since the mid-'60s artists, artisans, and students have joined families seeking affordable rent to make a richly diverse, revitalized community.

OPPOSITE

After years of organized lobbying by parents and kids, Friends of the Berkeley Skate Park worked with the city to create an impressive place to skateboard. Flooding in the rainy seasons closes it down due to seepage, but kids jump the fence anyway.

OPPOSITE INSET

A placid Buddha watches over the architectural elements at Omega Salvage's two surplus yards where you can find plumbing fixtures, decorative details, and ornamental iron-work—true antiques, not replicas.

ABOVE

A handler wrestles with an inmate at the East Bay Vivarium, the largest and oldest reptile retailer in the country on Fifth Street. The Vivarium offers a refreshing break from the high-end, man-made material culture a block west, into the primordial world of amphibians and arachnids.

LEFT

Tavera Early works in the garden at Berkeley Youth Alternatives. BYA serves South and West Berkeley youth with programs in tutoring, sports/fitness, arts, and job/life skills.

Gardens, Paths, and Parks

Berkeley has smaller parks than Tilden in the hills and the flatlands, although they are sometimes a bit hard to find—tucked in canyons and near the creeks (Strawberry, Live Oak Park, Cordornices), and along the waterfront. You can play soccer, baseball, basketball, disc golf, bowl on a lawn, or toss a Frisbee. You can walk your dog off-leash, and come upon the amazing paths built between roads winding in the hills. Two botanical gardens, in Tilden and Strawberry Canyon, delight gardeners with plant sales, inspiration, and solitude. Several parks (Martin Luther King, Live Oak Park) host festivals that strengthen a feeling of community in this college town on the Bay.

ABOVE

Cal's Botanical Garden features native, rare, and endangered plants and trees from around the world. Set in protected and quiet Strawberry Canyon, it is home to an exceptional cacti garden.

RIGHT

Friends of the Regional Parks Botanical Garden maintain this sanctuary of California rare and endangered native plants. The group grows species not known horticulturally, experiments with propagation and preservation, and promotes understanding of California natives through classes and lectures.

CLOCKWISE FROM THE TOP

Neptune keeps watch over swimmers at Willard Pool, part of the park adjoining Willard Middle School. All school pools in Berkeley have many hours available for community swimmers. • A member of Berkeley's Lawn Bowling Club delivers the bowl on Drake Green, dedicated in 1929 at Acton and Bancroft Way. Lawn bowling leagues exist throughout the Bay Area. • Girls play softball at Grove Park. Teams from several leagues compete in active high school softball.

OPPOSITE

A path stretches down to a road; walkers explore a woodland path between streets. The 150 footpaths were built to give a way for pedestrians to walk from homes to the key route transit system before there were many cars and roads. They are maintained by Berkeley Path Wanderers Association.

OPPOSITE

Soccer players practice at Cedar-Rose Park, built on five acres of the abandoned Santa Fe Railroad. Near the playground is Ala Costa Center, started by Berkeley parents 30 years ago to empower children with developmental disabilities.

LEFT INSET

A dog and owner pass under hanging cypress limbs near ball players in San Pablo Park, Berkeley's oldest park.

BELOW

Dogs have fun off-leash at the dog park on Hearst. It is part of Ohlone Park, 10 acres of open space and playgrounds near the North Berkeley BART station.

Architecture

Berkeley architecture before the 1900s is dominated by pockets of Victorian homes, colonial Revival houses with intact facades, bracketed Italianates, Queen Annes, and Stick-Eastlake houses and cottages. Berkeley residents adore the Craftsman bungalows and Brown Shingle houses built by Greene and Greene, Bernard Maybeck, and Julia Morgan.

For many Berkeleyans these Arts and Crafts style houses have come to define architecture here. Other major architects in the East Bay were John Galen Howard (Beaux-Arts-style) and John Hudson Thomas (Prairie Style buildings). The area northeast of campus has amazing houses: the Beaux-Arts neo Classic "Temple of the Wings," built by A. Randolph Monroe, and Hume Castle, by John Hudson Thomas.

The fires of 1923 and 1991 destroyed many homes, which have been rebuilt. Today many buildings and homes with a 21st-century touch can be seen in the flatlands and hills of Berkeley.

RIGHT

Storybook Tudor homes like this one on Benvenue in the Elmwood have been well preserved and creatively landscaped.

CLOCKWISE FROM THE TOP

An original stained glass window from 1900 on the second floor of the McCreary-Greer House (below), home of Berkeley Architectural Heritage Association. • Robin's Sandwich Shop has been a favorite of the Berkeley police department and other downtown city employees for almost 30 years. The Mother Goose or Storybook structure was originally built in 1946, as a gas station. • The McCreary-Greer House on Durant Avenue is one of the finest standing Colonial Revival homes from the late 19th century.

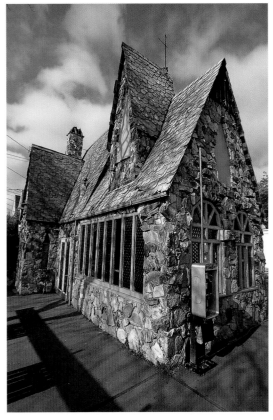

CLOCKWISE FROM THE TOP

The First Congregational Church of Berkeley was built in 1927, in classical red-brick New England style. The Church's Georgian interior holds more than 700 people and sponsors a performance and lecture series. • Julia Morgan's marriage of California Mission style with Mediterranean and Moorish design shows in this Elmwood house; painted figurative panels transform poured concrete from mere shelter into a habitat for the soul. • A stately Nordic-style home with pitched roof and fluted chimney cuts a geometric form against the blue California sky

OPPOSITE

North Berkeley has dozens of brown shingled homes— craftsman beauties—with hand-painted Arts and Crafts accents distinguishing their exteriors.

RIGHT

A close-up of the rustic Brown Shingle church, which is now The Julia Morgan Center ... a contrast to her Italian Renaissance City Club on Durant Avenue.

Julia Morgan utilized many of her personal talents learned in Europe when she built private homes for her clients. This "concrete" house on Claremont Avenue from 1926 has an interior courtyard with columns, and an Italianate fresco painted by a Coit Tower muralist.

JULIA MORGAN

CAL GRADUATE JULIA MORGAN casts a long shadow over the built environment of Berkeley. San Francisco-born and Oakland-raised, Morgan completed her engineering studies at Berkeley and headed for Paris, where she became the first woman to be granted a certificate from L'École des Beaux-Arts in 1902.

Back home, she worked with John Galen Howard on a huge master plan for the Berkeley campus. She opened her own firm in 1905, and for the next 35 years designed buildings and homes during the creation of suburban tracts in Oakland and Berkeley. Her public buildings include Hearst Gymnasium (with Bernard Maybeck), the Greek Theater (with John Galen Howard), the Baptist Divinity School, The Berkeley City Club, and St. John's Presbyterian Church, now the Julia Morgan Center for the Arts, all brilliant architectural structures.

CLOCKWISE FROM THE TOP

Walking is the best way to view lovely architectural details such as this sunflower wood carving found on a farm house bungalow in West Berkeley. • A hilly pair of craftsman-style residences shows a commonality of styles. • The church of Christ Scientist is a fine Maybeck building—here bedecked by wisteria.

An original Maybeck garage with room on top. The theatrically peaked roof behind dense foliage, rough-hewn native wood, and charming slim windows mark these updated carriage houses.

Cultural Life and Festivals

The cultural life of Berkeley is found in bars, night clubs, and community centers; in tony theaters, coffee houses, and dance venues; and in recording studios and on the air. From 924 Gilman's punk scene to the latest salsa club, Berkeley folks step out to experience artists and musicians who create poetry, dialogue, theater, comedy, and music to ponder or dance up a storm to. Once the rains have gone, this spirit spills over outside in fairs and festivals. World Music Festival, the Arab Film Festival, Solano Stroll, Indigenous Peoples' Day, Berkeley Free Folk Festival, Live Oak Park Fair, and Juneteenth are just a few. We kick up our heels, act silly, dance to great music, and celebrate being alive among others.

A Latin band performs at La Peña, the South Berkeley center for cultural exchange, which features international films, music, speakers, and programs for children.

CENTER

The Bobs strike up a great moment at Freight and Salvage Coffee House, which showcases a variety of music groups, including jazz and . blues, swing and big band, a cappella, folk, and solo comedians and story tellers.

TOP INSET

Raising the roof at Ashkenaz, a music and dance community club. Popular dance forms (an hour of lesson before the show) are Cajun, Caribbean jazz, Balkan dance and music, West African, and Latin hip-hop.

BOTTOM INSET

Broadcasters on-the-air at KPFA, founded in 1949, the first listener-supported radio station in the U.S. and member of the Pacifica group of indendent radio stations. Programming is local, original, and eclectic, in news, public affairs, arts, interviews, and reviews.

ABOVE INSET

Saul Zaentz in his office at Fantasy Records and
Films. His career as record and film producer
reached its height in 1996 with the receipt of
nine Oscars for *The English Patient* and the
prestigious Irving G. Thalberg Memorial Award.
Fantasy's recording studios, editing, and
sound-mixing facilities are used by Hollywood,
international and local filmmakers, as well as
his own company.

RIGHT

An audience at intermission at Zellerbach Hall
on the U.C. Berkeley campus. Offerings in
world and classical music and dance bring
audiences every weekend, with literary and
political speakers throughout the week.

LEFT INSET

Celebrating his 25th year of conducting, Kent Nagano is shown with members of the Berkeley Symphony Orchestra. This professional orchestra performs new and well-known masterpieces at Zellerbach Hall on the U.C. Berkeley Campus.

ABOVE

Under the artistic direction of Elizabeth Godfrey, Berkeley City Ballet trains young dancers for entrance into major dance companies. Here the Sugarplum Fairy and her Cavalier perform in the holiday *Nutcracker*.

LEFT INSET

Part of How Berkeley Can You Be is Harrod Blank's Art Car West Fest, a roundup of over 80 flamboyantly decorated cars, which display and compete, in a touch of pop culture American vernacular.

OPPOSITE

Musicians playing at City Hall in this festival celebrating the weird and wacky, which brings some 15,000 people and 90 participating organizations together.

BELOW

Circus characters on their float at How Berkeley Can You Be, a festival and parade started in 1996 to boost sagging morale on University Avenue, Berkeley's primary gateway.

CLOCKWISE FROM THE TOP

Browsers peruse Telegraph crafts booths. Twice a year the Avenue closes to cars, in summer for the Telegraph Street Fair. • A band plays at Earth Day, 2003, a fair drawing about 6,000 people sponsored by the city at Martin Luther King Civic Center Park. • A Berkeley policeman on bike near fanciful cars exhibited at How Berkeley Can You Be.

Fair-goers listen to an Earth Day band. Over 150 organizations display eco-friendly products and draw attention to environmental issues.

ABOVE

The ornamental gates at the Judah L. Magnes Museum, on Russell Street, which collects, preserves, and exhibits arts and artifacts reflecting the diversity and complexity of the Jewish experience throughout history.

CLOCKWISE FROM THE TOP

A mother and daughter pause before a colorful booth at the Himalayan Fair at Live Oak Park which showcases dance, music, and crafts from Asian mountain cultures. • In a choral moment at a recent Watershed Environmental Poetry Festival in Martin Luther King Park poets (left to right) Robert Haas, Michael McClure, Jerome Rothenberg, and Homero Aridjis read from Aridjis's *Eyes To See Otherwise*. • A tyke follows mom at Jazz on Fourth, a one-day outdoor jazz extravaganza to raise funds for Berkeley High School Jazz Ensemble and performing arts programs.

The Waterfront

Berkeley's waterfront is defined by the basin of the tranquil lagoon in Acquatic Park, created by streams that empty into it on the hill side of Interstate 80. Across the freeway the reclaimed shoreline that juts out at University Avenue sports a Marina and boatyard, Adventureland (a children's playground), restaurants, and the Marriot Hotel, the Berkeley Fishing Pier, and César Chávez Park. The soaring pedestrian and bicycle bridge built in 2001 leads across the freeway to this public-access shoreline.

OPPOSITE

The annual Berkeley Kite Festival at César Chávez Park has been flying high since 1986. It has become one of the three top kite festivals in the country.

LEFT INSET

When the winds are quiet, facing west to the Marin Headlands and Golden Gate Bridge with a morning paper is a great pleasure.

CÉSAR CHÁVEZ PARK

THE PARK WE PLAY IN was for many years the town garbage dump. Dikes were built in 1957 to contain and hide from public view a huge and sprawling dump, which became a land-fill operation. As attitudes changed during the '60s to value more highly this pristine piece of shore property, city fathers sought advice from Golden Gate Audubon Society and the Sierra Club, and crafted the Marina Master Plan in 1969. After hauling away tons of refuse, three feet of topsoil was "planted" covering the landfill. The site was fitted with an underground gas collection piping system to handle decomposition emissions.

Opened in 1991 as North Waterfront Park, it was renamed in 1996 to honor United Farm Workers founder César E. Chávez. The western rocky shoreline and protected wetland areas on the north surround planted vegetation of cypress and pine trees, fennel, mustard, dock, and coyote brush.

BELOW INSET

Adventure Playground, across from the Marina looking back at Berkeley, has delighted children for 26 years. Kids are free to hammer, saw, and paint forts, boats, towers, and fanciful creatures.

RIGHT

A quiet moment at the Berkeley houseboat marina. The thriving waterfront community sits right next to yachts, working fishing boats, and small sail craft in the 1,000-berth marina boat basin.

OPPOSITE FROM THE TOP

A rower enjoys peacefulness near the freeway. Protected Aquatic Park is a perfect place for kayaking, Cal rowing teams, scullers, and canoers since the Bay is often too turbulent. • A girl aims for a disc golf metal basket at the 33-acre Aquatic Park fairway, established in 1978. The "Pebble Beach" of California's 77 courses, challenges include treacherous winds off the Bay and overhanging trees, with the bonus of estuary lakeside and lovely views. • The dock and boathouse at the estuary.

THIS PAGE

Built as a WPA project on Berkeley's original shoreline, Aquatic Park is a mile-long wetlands sanctuary for fish and migrating birds. It is bordered by peaceful willowy trails on the east and Interstate 80 on the west, and is a favorite place for t'ai chi and quiet walks.

ABOVE

A windsurfer tests the wind, looking south towards Emeryville. Windsurfing is especially popular at this spot and in Marin, near Larkspur Landing.

OPPOSITE AND LEFT INSET

Stretching far out into the Bay, the 3,000-foot Berkeley Pier was built in 1926 to accommodate a new Berkeley-SF commercial ferry service, which failed after the opening of the Bay Bridge. The City of Berkeley turned it into a municipal fishing pier, where anglers find perch, jack smelt, California halibut, striped bass, kingfish, starry flounder, and white sturgeon.

ACKNOWLEDGMENTS

All photos with the exception of the following © Copyright 2004 Kiran Singh.

Photos on p. 25 © Copyright 2004 Ira Lapidus.

Postcards (poster art *Kissing In Berkeley* on p. 25; *Sather Gate At Dusk* on p. 49, 1939 watercolor by Chiura Obata) from the Collection of the University of California at Berkeley, Gift of Robert Gordon Sproul © Copyright 2004 Berkeley Historical Society.

Photos on p. 103 of Kent Nagano © Copyright 2004 Ron Jones, courtesy of Berkeley Symphony Orchestra; and Berkeley City Ballet © Copyright 2004 Andy Mogg, used by permission of Berkeley City Ballet.

Photo on p. 85 of Tavera Early © Copyright 2004 Joleen Scarella, courtesy of Berkeley Youth Alternatives.

The following photos by Kiran Singh are © Copyright the University of California 2004: Zellerbach Auditorium on p. 102, University Art Museum on p. 60, and Edith Kramer at Pacific Film Archive on p. 61.

Photo of Joyce Jenkins and *Poetry Flash* on p. 34, © Copyright 2004 Robert Schneck.

Watershed Festival photo on p. 109 © Copyright David Pang.

Drawing of The Cheese Board on p. 65 © Copyright Ann Arnold.

Historical photo of Tilden Carousel on p. 78 © Copyright 2004 East Bay Regional Parks District.

All other historical photos in sidebars © Copyright Berkeley Historical Society: #001 Bishop Berkeley on p. 21; #01416 People's Park on p. 26; #2353 Free Speech movement on p. 51; #3524 Elmwood Pharmacy on p. 45; #1199 Rose Garden on p. 70; #2077 Oceanview on p. 83; #4082 Berkeley City Club on p. 97; and #0068 Berkeley Marina on p. 112.

We are grateful to Tom Edwards and Berkeley Historical Society for the use of these photos and photo research, as well as to the organizations above who provided photos.

Kiran Singh's art photography has appeared in numerous art and media publications.

Ellen Weis is a writer and publicist based in Berkeley.

Michael Chabon's third novel, *The Amazing Adventures of Kavalier and Clay* won a Pulitzer Prize.

Sailboats caught in misty relief against the Marin hills at sunset sit timeless, on a shimmering sea.